CHICKEN

PUMPKIN CARVING STENCILS

HOW TO USE THE STENCILS

The patterns in this book are both easy and challenging.
The black-colored part of the pattern is the part to cut out from the pumpkin.

Step 1

CLEAN OUT THE PUMPKIN FIRST, SCARPING THE FLESH THINNEST IN THE REGION IN WHICH YOU WILL CARVE THE DESIGN

Step 2

CHOOSE A PATTERN AND CAREFULLY CUT OUT THE SHEET FROM A BOOK

Step 3

CUT OUT COARSELY AROUND THE PATTERN USING SCISSORS

Step 4

STICK THE TEMPLATE TO THE PUMPKIN WITH TAPE. USE A PENCIL TO MARK CLOSELY SPACED HOLES ALONG THE STENCIL LINES, PIERCING THE PAPER.

Step 4

CAREFULLY CUT OUT ANY PREVIOUSLY TRACED LINES USING A KNIFE OR A SPECIAL PUMPKIN CARVING BLADE

Step 5

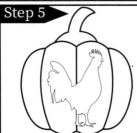

PLACE A CANDLE OR BATTERY POWERED LIGHT ON THE INSIDE AND ENJOY!

Made in United States
North Haven, CT
16 October 2022